It's Thanksgiving!

by Tessa Kenan

BUMBA BOOKS™

LERNER PUBLICATIONS ◆ MINNEAPOLIS

Note to Educators:

Throughout this book, you'll find critical thinking questions. These can be used to engage young readers in thinking critically about the topic and in using the text and photos to do so.

Lerner Publications Company
A division of Lerner Publishing Group, Inc.
241 First Avenue North
Minneapolis, MN 55401 USA

For reading levels and more information, look up this title at www.lernerbooks.com.

Library of Congress Cataloging-in-Publication Data

Names: Kenan, Tessa.
Title: It's Thanksgiving! / by Tessa Kenan.
Description: Minneapolis : Lerner Publications, [2017] | Series: Bumba books—It's a Holiday! | Includes index.
Identifiers: LCCN 2016001013 (print) | LCCN 2016005133 (ebook) | ISBN 9781512414295 (lb : alk. paper) |
    ISBN 9781512415018 (pb : alk. paper) | ISBN 9781512415025 (eb pdf)
Subjects: LCSH: Thanksgiving Day—Juvenile literature.
Classification: LCC GT4975 K45 2016 (print) | LCC GT4975 (ebook) | DDC 394.2649—dc23

LC record available at http://lccn.loc.gov/2016001013

Manufactured in the United States of America
1 – VP – 7/15/16

Expand learning beyond the printed book. Download free, complementary educational resources for this book from our website, www.lerneresource.com.

Table of Contents

Thanksgiving Day

It is Thanksgiving Day.
People celebrate this
holiday in the United
States.

Thanksgiving is in fall.

The harvest is in fall.

Food is gathered from farms.

Thanksgiving is a time of thanks.

People give thanks for the harvest.

What else might people give thanks for?

Families gather for a big meal.

They give thanks for their food.

They enjoy time with family.

Families eat different foods.

Many families eat turkey.

What other foods might people eat at Thanksgiving?

Pumpkin pie is for dessert.

People put whipped cream on top.

It is a tradition.

After the meal, some people volunteer. They share and serve food with others.

Why might people volunteer at Thanksgiving?

17

Some families play football.

Some families watch football

on TV.

Some people watch a parade.

How do you celebrate

Thanksgiving?

21

NOVEMBER

SUNDAY	MONDAY	TUESDAY	WEDNESDAY	THURSDAY	FRIDAY	SATURDAY
		1	2	3	4	5
6	7	8	9	10	11	12
13	14	15	16	17	18	19
20	21	22	23	24	25	26
27	28	29	30			

Thanksgiving comes once a year.
It is on the fourth Thursday in November.

Picture Glossary

celebrate

to do something fun on a special day

harvest

a time when food is gathered from farms

parade

an event that happens on the streets to celebrate a special day

volunteer

to help others without being paid

Index

Read More

Erlbach, Arlene. *Thanksgiving Day Crafts.* Berkeley Heights, NJ: Enslow Publishing, 2015.

Lawrence, Elizabeth. *Celebrate Thanksgiving.* New York: Cavendish Square Publishing, 2016.

Pettiford, Rebecca. *Thanksgiving.* Minneapolis: Jump!, 2016.

Photo Credits